Children's Books
and Class Society

Past and Present

Robert Leeson

Edited by the Children's Rights Workshop

Papers on Children's Literature No. 3

◉ **Writers and Readers Publishing Cooperative**

Introduction © Children's Rights Workshop
Children's Books and Class Society Past and Present ©1976 Robert Leeson
What were we arguing about? ©1977 Robert Leeson.
Published 1977 by Writers and Readers Publishing Co-operative,
233a Kentish Town Road, London NW5 2JT.
Cover illustration by Lee Robinson.
Printed and bound in Great Britain by Staples Printers Ltd, Rochester, Kent.

Contents

Introduction
page 1

Children's Books and Class Society Past and Present
page 9

References
page 47

What were we arguing about?
page 49

Further reading
page 59

Bob Leeson is literary editor of the *Morning Star* and he writes for children and for and about the Labour Movement. He has written:

For Children
Beyond the Dragon Prow Collins/Lions paperback 1973
The Third Class Genie Collins/Lions paperback 1975
The Demon Bike Rider Collins Young Fiction 1976
The Trilogy:
Maroon Boy Collins 1974
Bess Collins 1975
The White Horse Collins 1977

About Children's Literature
'Boom' in *Signal* No 13
'To The Toyland Frontier' in *Signal* No 16, Jan. 1975
'What Were We Arguing About' in *Signal* No 20, May 1976 and reprinted here.
'The Spirit Of What Age? The interpretation of History from a Radical Standpoint' in *Children's Literature in Education* No 23, Winter 1976

For Adults
United We Stand: British Trade Union Emblems Adams & Dart 1971
Strike: A Live History of 1887-1971 Allen & Unwin 1973

Introduction

Faced by the mountains of printed paper that accompany our everyday lives today, it is increasingly difficult to appreciate the social and political role that the printed word — newspapers, pamphlets and books — has played, and continues to play, in history. And yet, we don't have to look very far for signs of the power of the printed word. The banning and burning of books is a frequent practice in many societies, and writers and publishers have been, and are vilified, jailed, exiled or killed. Writing and publishing has never been a neutral activity, even in today's glut.

Books for children likewise have played their part in political movements as well as becoming their victims, and since the very early writings for children, i.e. when children were first seen as a separate readership, there has been a lively interest, if not concern, in what the writings were actually saying to children — about life and society. And whatever your views about that life or that society, or about what makes them tick, one thing is certain. The content, the message of children's books has always been a major concern, not the fringe, irrational obsession that most modern children's book commentators would have us believe.

Of course what books for children say to children is important. Words do have meaning. And children, people, matter: so much is obvious. And yet, there is a significant body of people, well-informed and well-meaning, who seem to hold the view that it is unimportant what books say. A book is a book they say. And children are children. It is enough to write or read a book; the rest will look after itself. What is important is how the thing is written, shaped or presented. These arguments may be familiar, the important thing is that they are widely held.

The two pieces by Bob Leeson in the following pages come from within the children's book world, a world still gripped by the 'book is a book' philosophy, but basking in the comfortable realisation of ever-increasing sales and an inevitably growing readership. In *Children's Books and Class Society: Past and Present* Bob Leeson places all these factors in the context of a perceptive sweep over two centuries or so of children's publishing and reading. Bob Leeson gently reminds us in his consideration of his own reading and of the roots of his writer's craft, that all these concerns have a natural place in a dynamic history of the fast expanding world of children's literature. Clearly, literature and children matter: far too important to be left to themselves!

This booklet does not contain a systematic or sociological analysis of children's literature. That is being attempted elsewhere, and we look forward to the fruits of this welcome field of study. Nor are Leeson's pieces outposts of a particular sociological, psychological or even Marxist Leninist perspective on literature, although they are naturally informed of the work in those perspectives. Here, Bob Leeson has written from the inside, as a practitioner of children's literature, a critic, literary editor and recently as a writer for children. It is precisely his many years of experience of children, of books and of publishing that give his observations the depth and breadth that they have, and ensure their relevance to those involved, or interested in literature for children. And it is Leeson's commitment to more and richer literary experiences for children, a commitment to truth and to social change that give these writings a purpose and scope that all too often are strangely absent in discussions about children's books — to the bewilderment of the neutral observer. After *What Were We Arguing About?*, it will no longer be possible to claim literary, or aesthetic privilege in the face of commitment to children, to literature and to children's literature. Commitment is in us all.

Children's Books and Class Society: Past and Present is an original piece, an elaboration of a talk by Bob Leeson entitled *Class Values in Children's Books* given on 15.5.75 as part of the Summer Course 1975 *Bias in Children's Books*, tutored by Andrew Mann of Children's Rights Workshop, at

Goldsmiths' College, South London (School of Adult and Social Studies). *What Were We Arguing About?* was first published in *Signal, Approaches To Children's Books* No 20, May '76, one of a small number of small-circulation specialist journals. We are anxious that these important and stimulating pieces reach a wider audience than the contexts in which the pieces first appeared. We welcome the appearance of Bob Leeson's experience and commitment as No 3 in our Papers on Children's Literature, thereby introducing a historical, socialist and British dimension to a debate in which *Racist and Sexist Images in Children's Books* (Papers on Children's Literature No 1) and *Sexism in Children's Books: Facts, Figures and Guidelines* (Papers No 2) have already reached a wide audience.

Children's Rights Workshop
July 1977

Children's Books and Class Society
Past and Present

Not long ago a radical comic called *Aardvark*[1] published a comic strip account of the eviction of squatters by the authorities in Brighton. The story was told in words and pictures adapted from the final chapters of *Wind in the Willows*. The remarkable thing was how well the extract from this story beloved of four generations of child and adult readers fitted the real life episode — an exhibition of property owning hatred and fear.

There, lying below the surface of Kenneth Grahame's inspired animal fantasy, a thing seemingly complete within itself, are all the symbolic figures of the troubled years in which the book was published: a playboy aristocrat (Toad's remarkably like Edward VII); respectable though critical but ultimately loyal owner-occupying friends from the River Bank; and, out in the Wild Wood, fearsome half-glimpsed, unnumbered and undifferentiated Stoats and Weasels.

In 1908, well-to-do, intelligent people like Grahame, former secretary of the Bank of England, looked with apprehension at an uncertain future. Within two years Britain was swept by industrial and social unrest, involving mainly unskilled workers, the poor and unemployed. As one old Salford foundryman told me — 'At the time there were so many out of work they were squatting on waste ground putting up huts and tents — the press called them "land grabbers".'

'Whack 'em and whack 'em and whack 'em' said Toad and before long Salford dockers, Cornish tin miners, Staffordshire chainmakers and Welsh railwaymen had been whacked by police and specials and more than weasels were lying on the ground.

Now *Wind in the Willows* is a fantasy tale, like so many children's books, and we take a risk reading social significance into it. Though George MacDonald, greatest of the Victorian fantasy writers (and the most didactic) wrote, in the same year that *Wind in the Willows* was published: 'The fairy tale cannot help having some meaning ... everyone, however, who feels the story will read its meaning after his own nature and development: one man will read one meaning into it, another will read another.'²

Is it all then in the eye and mind of the reader? Perhaps that is true for an individual book, but not, I think, in a whole literature. Surveying children's books in general, one can see underlying them the preoccupations and values of the middle class. Even today, when the readership of children's books goes much wider, and the literature depends for its distribution and often its very existence on the support of the whole community through schools, libraries and bookshops, its chief influence is that of one section of society. The working-class majority may figure in children's books, but for the most part have done so as outsiders, not as

The Occupation of Toad Hall 1970's style . . . as seen by the radical comic *Aardvark*.

central figures. In themselves they have barely existed.

In his amiable *The Enchanted Places,* Christopher Milne speaks of the 'air of snobbishness' about his father's *When We Were Very Young.* He says that A.A.Milne was writing to 'entertain people living in the 1920s and those were the attitudes current at the time.'[3] He does not analyse the sort of 'people' concerned and there is an underlying assumption that 'people' means a certain sort. As with 'people', so with 'children'. In his *British Children's Books In The Twentieth Century*, Frank Eyre remarks that 'children may never be able to learn how the children of poor homes, with limited opportunities, difficult backgrounds really feel until one of them grows up and becomes a good writer for them.'[4] Millions of working-class children know from personal experience what such a life can involve. But for the purposes of the children's book they do not positively exist. Writing of Eve Garnett's *Family From One End Street*, Brian Doyle (*Who's Who Of Children's Literature*) says: 'In the late 1930s it made children realise that not all their contemporaries owned ponies, had nurseries or attended boarding schools.'[5]

Now as a child of the 1930s myself, I am positive most children knew full well their 'contemporaries' had none of those things, any more than we had the yachts and lakes of Arthur Ransome's *Swallows and Amazons* (1930).

It is hard on Mr Doyle or Mr Eyre, perhaps, to demand that they should write 'middle class' children all the time. Nevertheless, one must always consider what writers mean by 'people' or 'children', when they use the words. Only in this way can one reach behind the assumptions which are part and parcel of the whole history of children's literature.

But my main contention about the middle-classness of children's books is nothing new. Writing in the 1930s, the author of by far the best book on the subject, Harvey F.J. Darton in *Children's Books In England: Five Centuries Of Social Life*, puts it precisely:

'Children's books, written as such, have been in England almost entirely a product of the large, domesticated middle class', which he says, found its feet in mid-18th century. This was when publisher John Newbery, known as the 'father' of children's books in England, was active and at that time, says Mr Darton, books produced 'ostensibly to give children spontaneous pleasure' became the 'definite object of the activities of the book trade'.[6]

Children's books then have a two centuries history and a middle class history at that. This is not astonishing if we look at their pre-history, at the way in which commerce, literacy and printing developed in this country along with the rise of an ambitious class whose children were hopefully destined for higher things. Like the adult novel the children's book is part of that development, though this does not mean that the middle class invented the novel and children's literature.

To put it sketchily, what the middle class did was to take the traditional tale of pre-printing days, which blended all forms — moral, fabulous, fantastic, historic, heroic, comic — often in the one telling — and break up its roots for specialised planting out. This literary horticulture has today reached the point where some critics are prepared to treat message and meaning as weeds in the garden of the imagination.

From the ancient tale was taken the hero (or more rarely the heroine) who was changed from a symbolic, larger than life character who might represent the aspirations of a whole folk, into a private individual, ambitious but down to earth, realistic but mundane, whose struggles might be painful but would have a private end — one which was to become more and more trivial.

The existing wealth of tale, fable, legend, from which the makers of the children's book drew and still draw, accumulated over many centuries. Anthropologists reckon that certain tribes have an oral recollection of events over thirty generations (perhaps sevencenturies). In such recollection the strictly historical and the near fabulous may run together. Even today we see how certain wise or witty remarks are often attributed to well known people, when there is no proof they ever made them.

The oral tradition came to its climax in the feudal age. The small number of manuscript books that existed were often used for reading aloud (anyone who has travelled in the Middle East, say, will have seen young and old gather round a visiting student or teacher who reads aloud from a newspaper).

In the feudal age, society's layers were held more firmly in place by custom and regulations: the sumptuary laws which tried to determine the style of clothes for different social classes lingered on until nearly 1600. The prevailing notion was that the child should become what its parents were, as soon as physically able. Against this background the heroic or comic tale might offer a release from life's strains by fantasies of low triumphing over high, the just over the unjust, the low born lad winning half the kingdom, the small man killing the giant and the 'slow' farmer outwitting the Devil. (Some years ago I was entertained by a new version of Hans Christian Andersen's *The Tinder Box* in which a sensitive modern adapter, instead of having the dogs throw the king and queen in the air, had the rulers resign while the soldier took over the country. In political terms, innocently out of the frying pan into the fire.)

Along with stories told by older members of the community, or travelling 'devisers of tales', were jests and riddles, some as old as 1,500 years. These constantly refresh themselves as anyone who reads the Opies' *Lore and Language of Schoolchildren*[7] or John Wardroper's *Jest upon Jest*[8] may see. The story-tellers had no doubt that they were entertainers. If they did not entertain they lost their audience and their supper. But they were entertainers who dealt readily in moral too. Even today we recognise that the shortest joke must have a point. But in ancient days when the skald turned aside from his narrative to remark, 'Now that was a good king', no aesthete rose from the other side of the fire to protest at his didacticism.

That the audience for the tale was of all age groups we know from Sir Philip Sidney's remark: 'He cometh unto you with a tale which holdeth children from play and old men from the chimney corner.'[9] Though I would guess that as the evening wore on and the smaller members of the audience fell asleep, the content of the telling might change. And we know from those tales which remain, that a story often had layers of meaning to be divined according to your experience of life.

From *The Canterbury Tales* we know that different classes listened easily together, though Chaucer also makes it clear that the Knight, the Reeve and the Wife of Bath had different tastes in stories — perhaps those stories they might choose *had they been reading a book by themselves.* In Chaucer's time (late 14th century) courtiers might prefer a romance from the French. But we are still far from the aristocratic jeers at Bottom the Weaver and his fellow craftsmen-actors in Shakespeare's *Midsummer Night's Dream* (1594-96).

Still, a socially mixed audience would contain people who would draw different morals from *The Hunting of the Cutty Wren*, or *Jack the Giant Killer.* The every-day implications of the most fantastic tale, mingling historic and legendary figures and actions, were very great — and greater in times of stress. 'Devisers of tales' had power and in the late 14th century they could be jailed if they devised them to the discredit of the King and his ministers. Feudal authority sought to control the tale. The Church, likewise, controlled the manuscripts as much as possible, using saints' lives — as it used pilgrimages — to manipulate the political mind.

Minstrels got their charter in the 1480s from King Edward IV, who gave their guild special nationwide powers to expel from the profession 'rude husbandmen and artificers of various crafts', thus giving something of a class character to the profession. And not surprisingly when the printing press was established in 1476 (Edward IV being patron to Caxton as well as the minstrels) the same nationwide control was exercised over the new 'mystery' of type. Even after 150 years of printing, there were only twenty printers with an official licence.

But printing could not remain a monopoly any more than story telling could. And the story came to mean more and

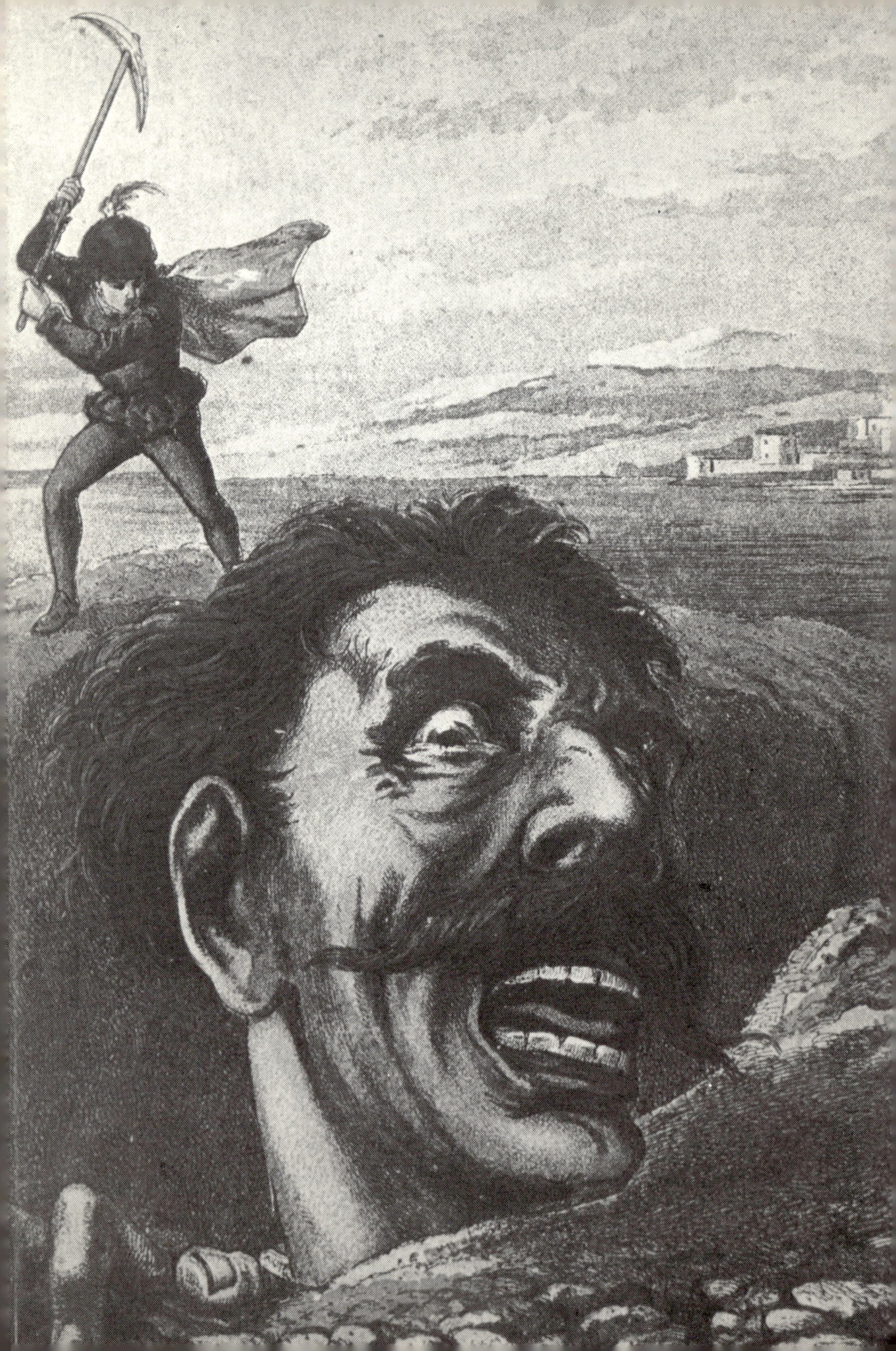

more the printed word. Among the first printed books were the fables and tales already popular. *Jack the Giant Killer, The Seven Champions of Christendom, Bevis of Hampton* (another giant killer) went into print along with *Renard the Fox,* Aesop, the French romances and collections of local jests and riddles. More rare were the Books of Nurture or Manners, aimed at instructing the children of the wealthy, in such books we begin to read a different note — a criticism of 'feigned fables' which bring mischief to youth. Those whose function it was to hold the higher reaches of society, had to distinguish between profit and pleasure.

Books became cheaper, more plentiful. The word 'pamphlet' is in use by the 15th Century. So print became a medium of power — and of subversion, an instrument in the class struggle in fact. A prolonged battle was waged around the new medium, centering on the right to print the Bible in English and put it into the hands of the congregation, not merely the priest.

The struggle continued through the 16th and into the 17th century, its Puritan heroes and martyrs suffering tortures and burnings for their beliefs until the Civil War and the rule of the Commonwealth that followed (1649-1660) put an end to Royal-Church control of the printing presses.

But more than the freedom to print was at stake. This was part of the wider social movement by the new class of merchants and master craftsmen, to break the power of the landowning nobility with King Charles I at its head. Once the King's forces, the 'Cavaliers', were defeated and the rigid feudal order was broken the way was laid open for the fuller development of the new social and economic order of capitalism.

To the merchant-craftsman class, the cadre force of the new era, freedom to speak, to read, to worship, were all entangled with the all-pervading freedom to trade and prosper in their own way for which they had fought. These

Jack the Giant killer in action, illustration from Routledge's Shilling Toy Book c. 1872.

people standing between the poor labourers of town and country and the aristocracy, were proud to be known as the 'middling sort'. They were, though, a 'middling' sort that intended to rise. Their religious ardour was blended with material ambition and a new approach to science and philosophy which laid the foundation to much of value in the centuries to come.

Their enemies called them indiscriminately 'Puritans'. It was intended as a term of abuse against all of them — noble spirits like Milton and militant democrats like John Lilburne, as well as the most narrow-minded overlookers of the human soul. It is as well to remember the original use of the word 'Puritan', employed so often these days in a narrow sense to mean censorious and restrictive. It is, though, perhaps inevitable that as time passed and the 'middling sort' got a taste of power, its rebel, reforming impulse began to fade and the mantle of 'Puritanism' remained with those who wished to control and not liberate.

At the height of the Civil War in 1644, the Puritan John Milton proclaimed to those in Parliament who wanted to restore the old censorship of the press — 'Give me the liberty to know, to utter and to argue freely.'[10] Under the Cromwellian Commonwealth, the total number of presses at work, swelled by pirate printers, rose from twenty to sixty, letting loose a storm of pamphlets, political and religious, prophecies and almanacs, books of Protestant martyrs to replace the saints' lives and cheaper versions of the old legends and ballads. The first edition of Aesop's Fables designed for the young was made by a former trooper in Cromwell's army.

In 1670 the 'Merry Monarch', Charles II, was restored to the throne. He rigidly controlled the press, with hanging for impertinent writers. His poet-censor Lestrange, whom his contemporaries likened to a dog, was more restrictive than any 'Puritan'. But the commercial pressures were overwhelming and by the 1690s the limits on the number of printing presses had been broken for good.

The Puritans were great educators. They aimed to reach out from the commercial and manufacturing centres of the

South East to 'civilise' the backward regions of the North and West by sending forth a host of preacher-lecturers, well armed with worthy books. For them the superstitions of both Catholic Rome and 'pagan' Wales were to be overcome with truth and light. Sense and science would drive out ignorance and nonsense. 'Feigned fables, vain fantasies' and what philosopher John Locke called 'perfectly useless trumpery'[11] in reading matter for any age group, were to be discouraged. What gave a solid base to Puritan rage against giants and dragons was the genuine feeling that those who even half-believed such things were prey to any deception.

Almost a hundred years later in 1766 the writer of *Goody Two Shoes* complained that children fed on a diet of such stories would 'continue fools all their days'.[12]

The twin drive against superstition and ignorance stimulated education and the uncontrolled growth of the printing press. The slow transition from social story telling to individual story reading began to separate the literate from the illiterate, the stumbling reader from the swift and the searcher after light from the seeker after pleasure. And in the minds of the educated, adult illiterates were equated with children. Experienced they might be, book learned they were not and book learning was what counted.

The gap between the didactic and the entertaining was opened, though then, as later, it proved difficult to separate them entirely. In John Bunyan's *Pilgrim's Progress* (1678) are mixed earnest didacticism, religious passion and the wildest 'feigned fables' of monsters and giants in our language. *Pilgrim's Progress* is one of our first novels and eventually a classic children's book. It shared the fate of many stories which once delighted all ages, sliding down the age groups until it reached the youngest. Bunyan's book also, as befitted the work of a former Cromwellian soldier, showed a sturdy independence of the rich and powerful. Some traces of this are to be found in *Goody Two Shoes*, although there the greedy landlord is offered repentance rather than hell-fire.

A new class had come to power, though, and set to work

to consolidate its new won positions through another three or four generations until as Harvey Darton says,[6] the 18th century began to confirm the security and 'domestication' of the middle class. To consolidate new won positions, the new social group prepared each generation to hold them. It educated its own. The guilds endowed grammar schools, and a new kind of book was designed for children destined not just to fill their parents' shoes but go higher if possible.

The slaying of dragons and giants does not inspire you to learn the law, buy your way into the livery company or even marry the master's widow and take over the workshop. Though an old legend grafted onto the life of Dick Whittington, thrice Lord Mayor of London between 1397 and 1420, might do just that. The romantic tale of Dick and his cat became popular 200 years after he died. The legendary tales, mingling the real and fantastic, were made more real, shifting the heroes nearer to the readership. Passing through a struggle for power and the accumulation of property to 'domestication', also meant the toning down and 'suburbanisation' of the heroes of the greenwood and meadow. Through the 17th and 18th centuries the loudest note was the stern one. The idea of a journey, fraught with temptation and danger and bounded by death was common. Janeway, the preacher-writer of the late 17th century, was typical of the era, and a sort of bogeyman in the pre-history of children's literature, with his exhortation to children to prepare themselves for death. Though one cannot help but admire the guts, no matter how narrow, of a man who stayed on in London during the Great Plague, nor fail to understand how real and close death was to him and his child readers.

But, while the 'middling sort' moralised their own social success, other forces were at work. The search for commercial profit led the small pirate printers to satisfy some of the needs of the lower orders. Free trade was for those with a penny as well as a pound, even if their share was but one two hundred and fortieth. To the cottage door came the hawker, the travelling salesman or 'chapman' with his load of books, turned out on the same machines which once poured out the religious polemics and the Leveller pamphlets of Commonwealth days. In the chapman's bag would be *Robin Hood* or *Guy of Warwick,* hymns and sermons, ballads, primers and adding up books, as well as political pamphlets and broadsheets, which achieved phenomenal sales in the 18th century.

The chapbooks varied in quality. They were often lurid. The oral tradition was dying (I say this with caution because tales were still being collected in the 20th century and I can remember men going round reciting nonsense poems in Lancashire pubs for free beer, only 25 years ago).

But while it died it was plundered by printers after a quick profit. The most popular tales were reprinted over and over and while ballads, jests and riddles were renewed to some extent well into the 19th century, the main stock of tales and legends was declining as the story tellers lost their custom and the way of life that inspired them dwindled away. The process of renewal no longer vigorously at work, the quality was vitiated by hack commercial reprinting. The root of the word 'chap' is the Norse 'kjøp' meaning 'to buy'. From it is derived the old word 'cheapen' meaning to bargain and lower in price, and thus the word 'cheap' which in the 19th century had already been linked with the word 'nasty'. But the chapbook kept alive the 'feigned fable' and thus plagued future generations of middle class moralists. The writer of *Goody Two Shoes* complained that 'people stuff children's heads with stories of ghosts, fairies, witches and such nonsense when they are young'.[11]

In the 18th century too, the still vivid folk fantasy tradition gained a crude urban reinforcement, with tales of footpads and gallows birds in publications like the Newgate Calendar, all feeding a turbid underground stream (as well as inspiring Defoe and Fielding) which flowed on into the comics and cheap paperbacks of our day and at all times has secretly entertained the children of the respectable.

Orthodox booksellers saw that the respectable were the main and most profitable market. For their children childhood was growing longer. The mid-18th century saw children of well-to-do families being dressed for the first time specifically as children. One may well imagine the effect of this lengthening of childhood and dependence, on the women of the family who were thus more and more tied to the home and separated from the running of workshop or business. The overcrowding of the city saw the merchant, the craft-master and the lawyer move their family houses to the suburbs increasing the family's separation from work and hastening the 'domestication' process. For such a 'suburban' market new books were needed.

In 1743, John Newbery published: 'A little pretty pocket book intended for the instruction and amusement of little Master Tommy and Pretty Miss Polly with an agreeable letter to read from Jack the Giant Killer as well as a ball and pincushion the use of which will infallibly make Tommy a good boy and Polly a good girl; to the whole is prefixed a letter on education humbly addressed to all parents, guardians, governesses, etc, wherein rules are laid down for making their children strong, healthy, virtuous, wise and happy.'[13]

Note the appeal to instruction *and* amusement. The new arrivals could afford in the words of the *Lilliputian Magazine or Children's Repository* to 'mix the whimsical, the witty and the moral'.[14] Rules were laid down to make the children virtuous and Jack the Giant Killer was offered as bait. In 1767 Newbery said that his character Tom Tripp was better than Tom Thumb, though no bigger, because he was a great scholar.[15] The mixing of the whimsical and the moral involved a degree of deception.

For the lower orders then the old stories, songs, ballads and the chapbooks. And if Francis Place's recollections of his 18th century childhood are accurate servant girls and apprentice boys were offered along with the pens and paper they bought in back street shops, a sight of 'pretty' pornographic pictures.[16]

But for the middle class there were its bookshops, its newly opened commercial libraries and now its own literature, created for its own children. It was a literature of a special character.

The change from a fairly rigidly defined society ruled by a landed aristocracy to one in which the economy was more and more based on trade gave this new class its opening. Land ties, money unlooses. So the middle class felt itself caught in a kind of social convection current which might raise up or cast down. They were filled with hope and determination and with apprehension at the same time. Great things might be won. In 1755, a book was offered as a present to 'every little boy who would become a great man and ride upon a fine horse and to every little girl who would become a great woman and ride in the Lord Mayor's coach.'

One has to note here that the way marked out for Tommy was different from that for Polly. Newbery's volume of letters from an uncle in 1788 warns Polly of a 'certain affectation that has lately stolen in on your behaviour of imitating the manner of the opposite sex.'[17] The specific subordinate role of women, which is not the main theme here, has been taken for granted in most children's books ever since. Susan Coolidge made sure that whatever Katy did next it was not climb trees[18] and Charlotte Yonge believed 'passionately in self denial and the inferiority of women'.[5] And in 1974 an author had her young hero 'sick at himself for playing at make believe like a girl.'[19]

In their different ways, Tommy and Polly read the new literature or had it provided for them by mother or governess and through their books they shared with their parents the hope of rising and the fear of falling. This was the bourgeois age. Trade and commerce opened the way up. But only a few could reach the pinnacle and live securely on their stock as the old style aristocrat lived on his broad acres. The middle class were conscious always of being the 'middling sort'. The master craftsman stood midway between the merchant and banker and the journeyman.

In 1720 the South Sea Bubble speculation collapsed and many lost their savings. The respectable family must have been very conscious of the two-way nature of social traffic and this experience may have been the starting point of that type of children's story which gained a new lease of life when I was a lad — where Roger's father has lost everything in the Slump and he must leave St Dominic's and go to a rotten day school.

Insecurities apart there was pride in being of the middling sort. 'Men of low degree are a vanity and men of high degree are a lie', sang the Psalmist.[20] There was value in being in the middle and it sustained you in the fight to reach the top or keep off the bottom.

Effort was the thing. Don't be dazzled by riches; be decently kind to the poor but watch your pockets. The notion of the lower orders as essentially delinquent is entangled with the fabric of the children's book to this day. Ask yourself how many children's stories you have read in which working-class characters appear as crooks to be outwitted by fearless middle-class children. Then, if you will, compare it with the number of stories in which fearless working-class children outwit middle-class crooks.

The middling sort were in an ambiguous position, looking aloft and over their shoulders at the same time. And this caused a certain contradiction between ideal and reality in their literature. In Thomas Day's *Sandford and Merton* (1780s) the poor farmer's son is virtuous, the rich merchant's son is spoiled. But for all that it is the spoilt boy who is going to inherit the family business. Some 130 years later, in *The Secret Garden*, Colin is a spoiled brat and Dickon a gradely Yorkshire working-class lad, but we know whom the heroine is destined for.[21]

In *The Kind Tutor* (1813)[22] we have a detailed, sentimental picture of how a spoilt young lord behaves. The long poem *The Dandy's Ball* (1823)[22] waxes satirical at the idle rich and another story tells the reader that 'the true course of happiness, remember' is 'in employment' (1825).[22] One may rise to the top but that means responsibility as we see from *Summer Rambles* (1820s).

'Harry: "What may I do that I may not be idle? I cannot dig you know I am not strong enough."

Mamma: "Nor is it needful you should. Your papa has money enough to pay people to work for him and a great many poor labourers live by what they get from him."

Harry: "Then I may be as idle as I please . . ."

Mamma: "No indeed you may not . . ."' and she goes on to describe the education that awaits him.[22]

In *The Pleasing Instructor* (1810) we learn how Pretty Polly the cottager's daughter becomes lady of the manor — just as Goody Two Shoes marries the squire and brother Tom comes home with a bag of gold. In another story a fine gentleman is reduced to a cottager.[22]

There are dangers in being naughty, children were told. In a poem called *The Crowd*, Sally wilfully runs away:

When alas! in a mean and dirty dark alley
Some women took hold of our poor little Sally;
Then instantly all her good clothes they were stripping,
And if she cried out, were preparing a whipping.[22]

Perhaps Charles Dickens borrowed this scene for *Dombey and Son* (1847). This fear of losing position or even identity, to emerge horrifyingly in a station lower than that one has been accustomed to is a recurring nightmare — Mark Twain made good satirical use of it in *The Prince and the Pauper* (1882). In one story a little boy is transformed into a chimney sweep. 'He made me take off my nice blue jacket and put on a nasty sooty coat. Look at my shoulder mama.'[22] On the other hand, Charles Kingsley's chimney sweep Tom is washed clean of dirt *and sin* as well, in *The Water Babies* (1863).

From here on a long line of children are plunged by circumstance into undeserved poverty. In more modern times, Edith Nesbit's *Railway Children* (1906) and *Treasure Seekers* (1899), stories which have been transformed by the talent of their teller, still spring from the same fount of inspiration. How a writer's talent can enliven such a tradition can be seen in Leon Garfield's books, *Smith* (1967) finding a new social status and 10,000 guineas at the end, or the heroes of *Devil in the Fog* (1960), *Jack Holborn* (1964) and more recently *The Sound of Coaches* (1974), find that their real identity is that of a different social order. It is the convection movement up and down through the social classes which provides the motion, suspense and tension of literally hundreds of children's stories old and new.

In the turmoil of the Industrial Revolution, millions were uprooted and among them tens of thousands of children, laughingly called 'apprentices' by the parishes who farmed them out. They were shipped by cart or barge load to the new hell of the textile mills or the peace of an unmarked grave. Small wonder the fear of loss of place and identity was a nightmare for families whom effort or good fortune had elevated.

And with the Industrial Revolution a new social force added grimmer figures to the nightmare — the industrial workers who owned nothing and owed nothing. In the red light cast across the Channel by the French Revolution they appeared even when seeking simple justice to threaten the whole way of life of the respectable. So new pressures emerged to affect children's upbringing and literature.

Educationists were divided into two camps. There were men like the Quaker Joseph Lancaster (1778-1838) whose educational system was eagerly adopted by some of the early trade unions. And there were people like Hannah More (1745-1833) and Sarah Trimmer (1741-1810) for whom schooling in the wrong hands led to sedition. Mrs Trimmer who fought the 'Lancastrians' tooth and nail, feared the effects on the working classes of the deadly combination of Revolution and education. She found 'much mischief' in children's books and has become a byword for 'puritanical' nose-poking into the content of children's literature.

But she was typical of her class and time. When John Shuttleworth, Secretary of the Privy Council for Education, advocated state aid to pay school teachers he said to the well-to-do who complained of such expenditure that they should realise how useful it was in keeping young people out of the wrong hands. Such people he said 'appear to forget how many thousand troops of the line are employed to protect the institutions of the country, how many thousand police to watch the houses and protect their persons — how many warders, gaolers and keepers of the hulks.'[23]

During the 19th century, some of the more skilled workers won leisure and prospects for their own children in a way that emulated the past struggles of the 'middling sort'. Like them the workers produced a new crop of martyrs for the freedom to print and organise. Men went to jail, or were transported for selling unlicensed newspapers. But most of the descendants of the old 'bible martyrs' had forgotten their origins and supported the prosecutions. Men like Thomas Hughes were an exception. The author of *Tom Brown's Schooldays* first and worthiest of the public school stories, was a consistent if paternalistic friend of the trade unions. But such notions as the right of workers to organise were not allowed to penetrate the nursery though harrowing tales of the fate of factory children did begin to reach the young reader.[24]

Those skilled workers who sought formal education were

Michael the child labourer on his day off.[24]

of course susceptible to the influence of the middle class. When they ran their own Sunday Schools as the Primitive Methodists, one of the more radical of the Nonconformist Churches, did, they had few books and often taught reading by traces in a sand-box. Such books as they acquired came from a publishing trade in capitalist ownership and staffed by the middle class, who supplied the values, the morals, the atmosphere and — above all — the authors.

Through the 19th century we see a group of middle-class writers emerging, who produced stories mainly or entirely for the children's market. When not writing books they contributed stories to the magazines designed for children which flourished in Victoria's time. They are a formidable band and they made a lasting mark on literature. When, in 1968, Brian Doyle produced his *Who's Who of Children's Literature*[5] he listed some 160 British authors (68 dead and 92 living) whose lives spanned two centuries and whose work was still available or even popular. Of 75 authors for whom any details of parentage are given, 26 were clergymen or their children and another 18 the children of stockbrokers, judges, service officers, manufacturers and government officials. Only nine were of distinct working-class origin. Of 125 whose education was described, seven were elementary school children, 100 were from private, boarding schools etc.

This does not mean to say that none of them were ever enabled by their talent to transcend their origins and produce literature of universal appeal. But it does mean that their origins and background were above all the source of inspiration of children's books from one generation to another.

Increasing middle class social stability, the lengthening of childhood in middle class families, the growth of the literature itself which stimulated the search for new forms reflected itself in a growing tendency and ability to 'mix the whimsical, the witty, and the moral', an ability to relax into nonsense and fantasy. The intellectual reaction against the gross materialism of the drive to industrialisation which expressed itself in the literature, art and music of the Romantic period, in children's literature led to the rehabilitation of those myths and fantasy figures the moralists had cast out. The fairy tale was reinstated, and not simply as a reaction to didacticism but as a positive aid to it — as Charles Kingsley demonstrated with *The Water Babies* (1863). Charles Dickens, so John Rowe Townsend reminds us in his book *Written for Children*, thought the fairy tale 'taught forbearance, courtesy, consideration for the poor and aged, kind treatment of animals, love of nature, abhorrence of tyranny and brute force'.[25] It had all the necessary ingredients.

Though, as Anna Sewell's *Black Beauty* (1877) and a host of later and lesser imitations suggested it was perfectly consistent to love animals and detest the brutal poor who always seemed to ill-treat them. The worst that could happen to horse as to human was to slide down the social scale.

The reinstatement of fairies and fantasies, the development in the later Victorian period of the nonsense story of the Lear-Carroll kind, gave to children's literature (or shall we say, gave back) the full range of elements which had been present in the old folk tale from the comic to the adventurous. But it must be said that nowhere was the sense of duty neglected. It became more embedded in stories of a set kind, the public school story and with the growth of empire the explorer-adventurer tale — the muscular heroes of George Henry (1832-1902). Haggard's blond aristocrat musing on the cowardice of 'servants',[26] Ballantyne's gorilla slaughterers whose moralisings were often skipped over by readers impatient for the blood and thunder.

These stories offered a means of confirming in each generation the unconscious acceptance of a certain type of person from a certain background as leader in any aspect of life. The blending of the conventions into a kind of ritual, an assumed background to excitement and adventure in the 'Empire' story, enabled the two most apparently opposed elements, the moralistic and the mindlessly violent to join together. The combination was powerful. The muscular upper class heroes and their endless victories over 'lesser breeds without the law', an outcome never in doubt however strenuous the battle might be, made for a confident, extrovert literature which filled many books and a succession of magazines.

It reached its 'peak' by the end of the 19th century in the works of Charles Gilson, governor of an army prison who wrote many books like *In the Power of the Pygmies* (1918) and *Held by Chinese Brigands* (1920) and those of Captain Brereton *With Rifle and Bayonet* (1900) still being voted a 'rattling good yarn' by the *Morning Post* in the 1920s. The essential features of this type of story were set out recently by Geoffrey Trease . . .

' . . . the British must always win. One Englishman equals two Frenchmen, equals four Germans, equals any number of non-Europeans . . . the common people subdivide into simple peasants, faithful retainers and howling mobs. The Cavaliers were a good thing. So were the French aristocrats except for their unfortunate handicap in not being English.'[28]

Between the crudities of this kind of historical-adventure, the genteel fantasy, and the delightful animal story, another type of writer was at work, looking anxiously on the one hand at the effete escapism of the rich, and on the other at the suppressed violence of the poor. George MacDonald, classic fantasy writer with a Presbyterian conscience, is also incidentally the first writer to attempt to bring a working-class hero to the children's story (Diamond in *At the Back of the North Wind*, 1871). Using the metaphor of the mine to symbolise both the subterranean threat to complacency and the nobility of those who labour, MacDonald in *The Princess and Curdie* (1882) has his spirit-lady address Peter, Curdie's miner father, in this way:

' "It is a great privilege to be poor . . . you must not mistake however, and imagine it a virtue. It is but a privilege and one also that like other privileges may be terribly misused." '[29]

Since the plot demands that Curdie the miner's son marry the princess, the lady assures Peter that he and his wife already have royal blood in their veins. MacDonald could not so blatantly cross the class barriers and the days of the farmer's son who won half the kingdom were long past.

MacDonald's story ends with an awesome prophecy of doom for the kingdom if the decadent way of life of the court is not abandoned. From here to Badger's strictures to the profligate Toad of Toad Hall 26 years later is but a short step.

By the 20th century the full range of genres within children's literature had been developed and since then nothing new by way of vehicle for moral or sentiment has appeared, though the variations on the old themes have been many and inventive. Historically the shape and content of children's books was determined by the changing needs and aspirations of the middle class. The upper and lower classes appeared in children's books through their eyes, a periscope view of the aristocracy/capitalist class, a helicopter view of the working class.

Children's books reflected their hopes and fears, fantasies and complacencies, the latter strengthened as their society at the centre of its empire seemed capable of limitless economic and technological advance. What had long ago been achieved at the cost of social strife, now seemed theirs by 'natural' law. The 'middling sort' had become 'people'.

With the 20th century came a series of shocks — the First World War, the Russian Revolution, tremors through the Empire, the Slump. The confident assumption that education and application would result in upward social movement was most severely shaken, whereas the possibility of loss of social position was all too real. Middle class people became more and more conscious of the presence and demands of the working class, not burrowing like MacDonald's gnomes, not lurking in the Wild Wood, but out in the open. While some reacted with increasing fear and hostility, of which books like Buchan's *Huntingtower* are a reflection, others saw with growing clarity the common interest of what the Labour Party constitution (1918) called 'workers by hand and brain'. One reflection of this was the campaigning by the Labour movement for a broader and more democratic system of education. A programme of what we today would call 'comprehensive' and further education was put forward as early as the end of the First World War, by Ernest Bevin at the Dockworkers' Annual Conference (London, 1918).

Increased education meant more children's books, more children's writers. The inter-war period saw the introduction of the children's library, with Eileen Colwell beginning her pioneering work around the time of the General Strike. We had no children's library, but I remember vividly the library box in school each month. You had to be very much in favour to get the latest Ransome, Milne or Lofting.

Reflecting the social changes of the 20th century, the whole range of children's writing underwent a change and it is interesting to see what happened to each genre.

The school story, essentially the public/boarding school story, marched on, ostensibly unchanged, into the 1940s. But its content had changed all the same or rather its context. In 1899, Kipling in *Stalky and Co* had introduced a new type of school hero who laughed at the more ridiculous expressions of the 'Empire' code, while striving to make it more meaningful. Frank Richards' *Greyfriars* with Bunter, Bob Cherry (and the new Indian sub-rulers 'represented' by Hurree Jamset Ram Singh), carried the process further, caricaturing itself more and more, playing the stock situations more openly for the comedy.[30] From 1950 Anthony Buckeridge with his Jennings stories has made the laughter paramount, the school simply the situation for the comedy. Interestingly the girl's school (if we ignore the outrageous St Trinian's) has tended towards the serious, either the didactic as in Antonia Forrest's books ('Yes, you know Nicole Marlow has the makings of a really capable team captain. She's really making those children work' — *The Cricket Term*, 1974) or the sentimentally escapist in the Chalet School.

While the old school story withered on the vine, postwar years have seen some vigorous off-shoots, Geoffrey Trease's *Bannermere* stories (1949-56), written deliberately

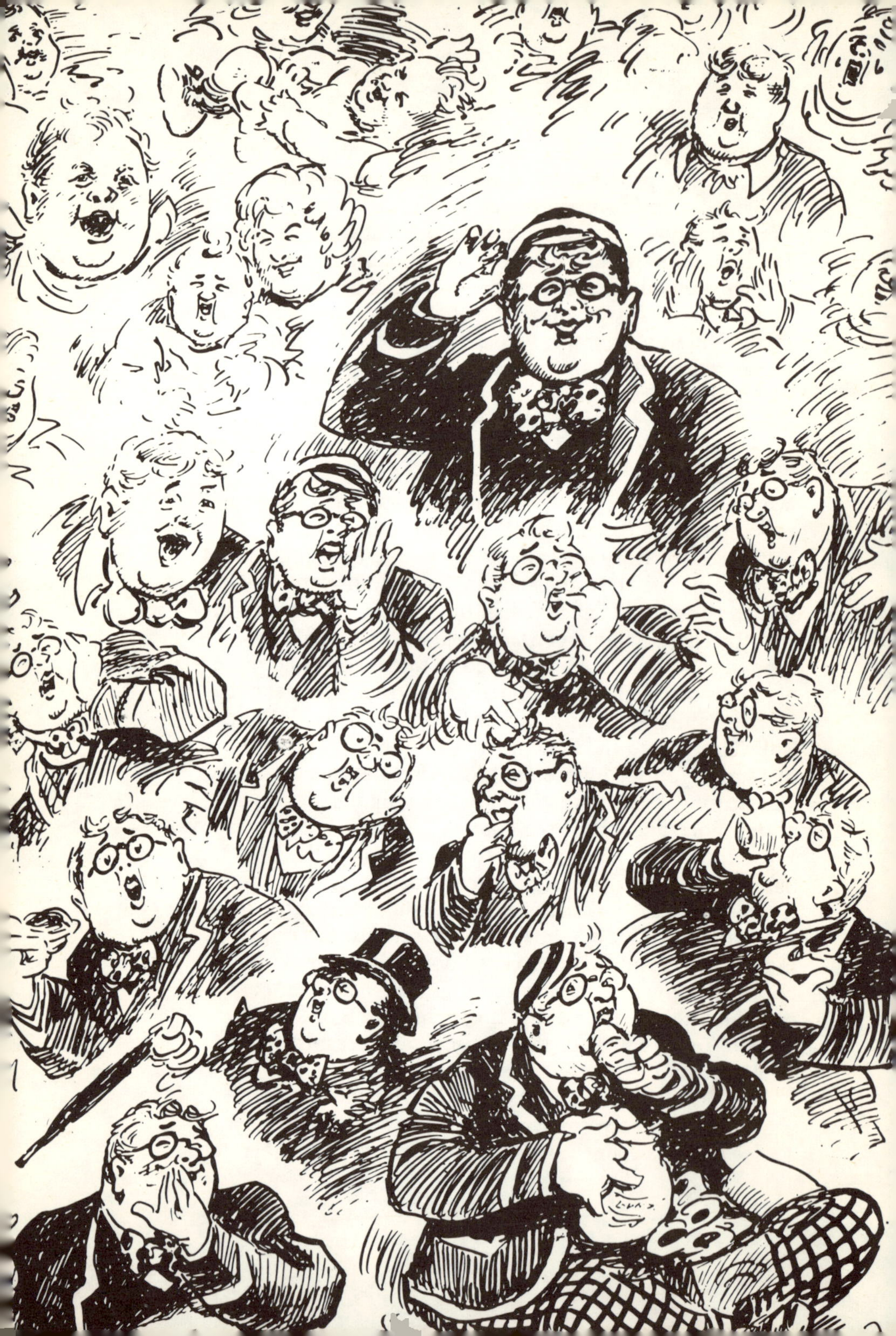

to provide books with a day-school setting. Closer to home, Wallace Hildick's *Jim Starling* books (1958-64) have been forerunners of a slowly increasing number of stories featuring the ordinary day school in an industrial town as the well realised, unselfconscious background to drama and comedy.

The modern school story must essentially come to grips with the life of working-class children and their home background, for the day school story (as I realised when I came to write my own *Third Class Genie* (1975) is the story of the community, and for the majority of day schools this is essentially the working class community.

The adventure-historical story almost came to a halt in its development with the First World War. Recalling what I read myself in the late 1930s, I note that only two titles out of 20 had been published in the previous decade. Eighteen of the titles were over 30 years old, 12 over 50 years old, eight over 75 and three over a hundred years old. As Geoffrey Trease remarked 'a new story in 1920 or 1930 tended to be a fossil in which one could trace the essential characteristics of one written in 1880 or 1890 . . .'[28]

It is interesting to quote Trease because his work beginning in the early 1930s marks a watershed in the historical adventure. In 1934, when he was writing serials for Boy's Own Paper, he also wrote *Bows Against the Barons* and *Comrades for the Charter,* starting a stream of books of which, as Frank Eyre says in *British Children's Books in the 20th Century,* 'concerned themselves as much with the social events of the time and their effects on the people who lived in them as with excitement and action.'[4]

Bows Against the Barons (1934) was rejected by orthodox publishers and Trease went with it to Martin Lawrence, forerunner of the Left Wing Lawrence and Wishart. This house also published Marxist writer Jack Lindsay's story of the Eureka Stockade, which had likewise been rejected

Billy Bunter of *Greyfriars,* a school story caricaturing itself. Illustrated by C H Chapman.

on the grounds that it showed a British officer 'in a bad light'.

It is not too much to claim that radical writers who have in mind the needs and aspirations of ordinary people today really set going the transformation of the historical and adventure novel and continue to enlighten it today.

In the Trease tradition we have had Peter Carter's *The Black Lamp* (1973), Audrey Coppard's *Nancy of Nottingham* (1974), *Time of Trial* (1963) by Hester Burton, Margaret Lovett's *Jonathan* (1972) and a number of others, though as any librarian knows it is easier to find novels about Roman Britain than about the Industrial Revolution and similar

'Dimly comic' Dustman Dad from Eve Garnett's famous *The Family from One End Street*.

periods in any library.

When we turn to the modern story we see how in the 20th century middle class writers have sought to widen their range of vision, taking in what are known as the 'less fortunate'. In the 1930s, the plight of East End folk in the Depression led Eve Garnett to write *The Family From One End Street*. Praised and awarded the Carnegie Medal, the annual book prize of the Library Association in 1937, this book is seen less kindly in perspective. It has been described by Brian Alderson of the Times who does not need me to assure anyone he is no revolutionary as 'reading like a dim comedy at the expense of washerwomen and dustmen';[31] although other critics see it as a story with 'authentic working class background'.[5]

Not every children's writer of course is guilty of seeing the working class as consisting mainly of chars and dustmen,

The 'less fortunate' working class as seen in *Gumble's Yard*. Illustrated by Dick Hart.

37

a kind of gigantic, but not very reliable service agency. But all too few have succeeded in viewing the working class from the inside. In the 1960s we had John Rowe Townsend's *Gumble's Yard* and *Widdershins Crescent.* Here we have the Eve Garnett sympathy but with far more subtlety and modern sociological understanding. But for all the subtlety and sympathy it remains an outside view. The young central figure still feels inadequate in face of the helpful curate and teacher who assist the family and their help leads him finally to this:

'The truth was I realised suddenly that Doris was simply not equal to things. She wasn't very bright or very energetic or very likeable.'

The achievement of his experience is to lead a working-class boy to a sympathetic, detached middle-class view of someone from his own household. It's not unfair criticism of John Rowe Townsend as a writer for children to say that he pushes this progressive, detached view of working-class life as far as it can go in our day and age.

Perhaps one should qualify this by saying that it is not working-class life which is being viewed but only a section of it, those of 'poor homes, limited opportunities, difficult backgrounds', referred to by Frank Eyre (page 2) that section of the working class which has excited the attention of a number of writers much as its violent-criminal section has excited other writers and continues to do in children's literature.

Working class life viewed from the inside in which the characters are given the dignity of a full existence, is much more a rarity in children's books. Those writers who have most succeeded in creating a genuine working-class background and characters are those who come from that background themselves, not 'less fortunate' people, but simply people for whom the whole way of life of the working class is a natural resource for their creativity. Written at the same time as *One End Street,* Eric Knight's *Lassie Come Home* (1940) for all its sentiment and deference is more convincing in its portrayal of dignified ordinary people. With Richard Armstrong's *The Mystery of Obadiah* (1943) and *Sabotage at the Forge* (1946), set in Tyneside factories his *Sea Change* (1948) about the merchant navy and *The Whinstone Drift* (1951) set in the mines we have authenticity plus a natural pride in work.

In this tradition in more recent years we have the short stories of Bill Naughton and the longer books of Catherine Cookson, *The Nipper* and *Joe the Gladiator,* Nina Bawden's village working folk and perhaps the most impressive in their dignity and independence the Scots characters of Allan Campbell MacLean. Dignity and independence are the key — the ability of such people to conduct daily lives which are rich and varied and not dependent on the mediation of their 'betters'. Though many writers still cannot conceive of

'Dignified ordinary people' in *Joe and the Gladiator,* illustrated by Gillian Shanks.

a group of working class children or adults actually solving a problem without assistance from higher quarters.

We have had a succession of Rider Haggard's Sir Henrys with their gun-bearers, John Buchan's lairds with their taciturn ghillies, W.E.Johns, Biggles and Gimlets with their trusty mechanics, and Malcolm Saville's public school boy 'born leader' with a loyal following of village children.

Sometimes the assumed social superiority is rammed home in an offensive manner. Thus Pamela Brown in *Golden Pavements* reissued in 1973: 'The decrepit chamber maid seemed incapable of calling them at the correct hour ... the waitress would infuriate them by serving watery haddock and cold toast at snail's pace.'

That one paragraph could be fruitfully analysed on its own as a rich example of snob assumptions and what they reveal about the assumers.

Or see how in Malcolm Saville's *Lone Pine Five* Mr Morton 'leaning on the bonnet of his car, lighting his pipe' puts down Smithson, who has 'grease glistening in his hair' and a 'vulgar abomination' of a scarlet and yellow tie. Smithson was furious, but 'he was no match for Mr Morton who pretended at first not to notice him and then not to hear or understand what he was saying'. Another effortless goal for the old school.

Nor do you have to be adult to put down the lower orders. Watch young Julian at work, with Enid Blyton's approval in *Five Run Away Together.* Having injured the Stick's son he grossly insults the father. Not the way a Victorian writer would have brought up her literary children.

Open snobbery, flaunting of real privilege or imagined superiority is rarer in children's books than it was. What persists however, often unconsciously, is the use of a phoney 'realism' in dialogue which by the use of phonetic spelling implies that only certain people actually pronounce words as they should be spoken. In Eve Garnett's *Further Adventures of the Family From One End Street* (1956) lovable Kate mispronounces her words and the author carefully underlines this. But Mrs Ayredale Eskdale does not. She may be a bitch but she knows the Queen's English.

In Noel Streatfield's *When the Siren Wailed* (1974) Laura says 'flars' for flowers, but Mrs Gregson who evidently comes from an accentless part of the world makes no such mistakes. It is literary illusion that all middle class people speak words with a perfectly neutral accent, as written. To my uncultivated ear, much speech by middle-class people sounds like the quacking of a duck, and it is a great temptation in my own writing to have such people say 'naice' and 'quaite' and pronounce butter as if it were a mixture of flour for frying, and a cup of tea as though it were something to wear.

But it's a pointless subjective exercise, for the true difference between characters of different social backgrounds lies not in pronunciation but in idiom, the choice of phrase or word. In such a cunning use of expression the author can impart a sense of social difference without demeaning the character, and it is by such crude devices as 'phonetic' spelling that authors betray their own distance from the characters they portray.

The truly successful writer, for adults as for children, is one who transcends the limits of accurately observed personal experience so as to say something of appeal for all readers. Few can do it, and those who do, remain in print (at least in children's books) for a very long time. But a literature is not made by truly successful writers alone, but by a great range of them, from the awful, through the mediocre, to the excellent. This is very true of children's books where the range of quality and subject is staggering.

That in all this variety the dominant values, background, atmosphere and mood is that of the middle class is a heritage left us by long history. Many of the welcome and progressive developments already noted in fact represent the seeking of middle class writers to come to terms with the new situation in which the class finds itself by the late 20th century.

In the world of education and children's books, some writers, editors, teachers, librarians, have shown themselves aware of the social limitations of much that is written and published. Their view is not that these limitations are 'natural' or even defensible, but that they should be overcome and that we should see ways and means of doing it. This change of attitude underlies the current debate about bias in children's literature.

But there are yet others who see this critique as a threat to all they hold dear and lump together the various groups of critics of class, racial and sex bias as seeking to put an end to all free, imaginative and creative writing for ideological and didactic purposes of its own.

Now the use of that term is partly based on a misunderstanding of the historical nature of puritanism. But there is an important grain of truth in the assertion. For as I argued earlier, the origins of children's literature lie in that 'puritan' period when feudalism gave way to capitalism, when a new social system brought new classes to the fore, not least the middle class which sought by education and other means to consolidate a new-won position.

Historically, today, we are in an analogous situation. Today a new class presses to the fore rejecting its assigned inferior role. If one judged from letters to the Times, the working class is now master of the land with the middle class lying wounded at its feet. No one has to accept that view to recognise that large-scale social changes are in progress, an old order is under pressure from a new. Yet even as we compare the social revolution of three centuries ago with the one which is now shaping up, we must note one over-riding and essential difference in the forces involved.

In the 17th century, one set of property and exploitive relations was exchanged for another. The troopers in Cromwell's army were told that they would have a say in the ruling of the country only if they had 'estate', a 'stake in the kingdom'. To which they replied that they had no estate but had 'ventured' their lives. Venture was a word used at the time for the risking of capital by investment, and the troopers' play on words was deliberate.

It compares with a story my father used to tell of an argument in which someone had spoken to him of the amount they had invested in the firm where he worked, and he had replied: 'Yes, but I've invested 35 years of my life.'

The former social revolution accomplished a change in the manner of exploitation and dominance. That social revolution which is now in question can only succeed if it aims not to create a new dominant group, but to replace competition with cooperation, not to elevate one sort above another, but to achieve a common interest among workers by 'hand and brain' in an undivided society.

Such a social change should mean not the supplanting of the literature of one class by the literature of another, but the achievement of a universal literature to reflect the drive to remove social distinctions and end exploitation.

Already in embryo we see something of the contradiction between the new and the old, between the class nature of children's books and the fact that the present and future of this branch of literature, through the library and school network, the bookshops, the parents and other organisations, lies in the hands of the whole community, a community within which middle class people, however active and talented, make up a minority. The majority of the community and its way of life and outlook are as yet insufficiently reflected in children's books. The middle class child can gain the full range of experience, excitement, amusement from all kinds of books. For the working class child far too many of the books are at one remove, in character and setting.

It is argued that the working class child does not want 'only to read about itself' and likes to escape into a different world in its reading. This is true, but only half the truth. For a full range of reading experience, the reader needs to identify, to recognise himself or herself, as well as to escape and have vicarious pleasure or thrills. Middle class children already have this provision built into a wide choice of books, working-class children much less so.

This critique of some of the more extreme forms of class bias in children's books — what is its immediate object?

Is it, as some people seem to fear, to expel the middle class writers from the field or to condemn them to concentrate on problem children in back streets? No indeed. Why should one want to exchange mediocre pony books for mediocre football books, made more mediocre by second or third hand experience of the subject matter?

Let writers write of what they know, but let them honestly consider how well they know their own world and how well their writing reflects changes which have already taken place in the world around them.

And let the children's book world be alert and responsive to find new writers as a new generation comes forward. Already in the teachers' and parents' organisations one can see people at work whose dynamic springs from the fact that they come from a working-class background. Where they are, the writers will be also, provided that it can be known to them that this is a field of writing which needs and wants their talents.

Alternative publishing on a local, and tentatively on a national scale from organisations like Centerprise of Hackney, has begun to influence children's books. More will follow. It will be said of this as has been said of the *Nipper* series of books which first set out in 1967 to challenge the hegemony of the *Ladybird* readers with their smooth suburban background, that they are 'self-conscious social engineering'. A similar self-consciousness by their own acknowledgement, motivated Geoffrey Trease and Wallace Hildick when they set out to renew the school story in the 1950s, but who today regards their work as 'social engineering'? Changes are taking place in the content and presentation of children's books the full import of which will not be appreciated for some years — when perhaps a proper comparison can be made between today and what has gone before.

Some publishers are making an effort to broaden their lists though not all efforts are equally valuable. For example the demands of teachers who are coping with the problem of the 'reluctant reader', have been responded to by publishers though often in a somewhat mechanical way. Series of books have been produced, some of which are superficially working class or 'urban' in background.

Many of the books, too, are superficially 'simple' in style, but in fact often shallow. Many are competent and may well help reluctant readers. But they should not be seized on as a 'way out' by publishers, and thus form a new second class or sub-literature while the mainstream, which has the publishers' most careful editorial and artistic attention, continues to cater for the old coventional readership in a somewhat updated way. It is perhaps too early to emphatically judge all this class of writing, but a warning note is certainly called for. Let us get it straight — what is needed is the transformation of the whole body of children's literature, not a phoney 'comprehensive' list of books with each category of reader covered at different levels.

The process will be a gradual one, seen from today's standpoint, but when one looks back at the enormous

From the 'smoothly suburban' world of a typical reader, to bouncily working class *Nippers* illustrated by Margaret Belsky.

development and expansion of the last two decades, one can see both the possible speed of future advance and the great potential for growth.

Running now at between 20 and 30 million volumes a year, children's book production could reach 100 million a year without giving every child of school age more than one new book a month to read. But such a production must be based upon a 'community market' not a narrowly sectional one. Within such a potential growth there is room for many sorts of writing. All the elements are present in small or large degree to make up a genuinely universal literature reflecting all aspects of life of all parts of the community.

The next thirty years development could match and even out-do the achievements of the past three hundred.

References

1. *Aardvark* (Aardvark Publications, Brighton, 1975)
2. *The Fantastic Imagination* by George Macdonald, 1908 (Signal Reprints, January, 1975)
3. *The Enchanted Places* by Christopher Milne (Methuen, 1974)
4. *British Children's Books in the 20th Century* by Frank Eyre (Longman, 1971)
5. *Who's Who of Children's Literature* by Brian Doyle (Evelyn, 1965)
6. *Children's Books in England: Five Centuries of Social Life* by Harvey F. J. Darton (Cambridge, 1958)
7. *The Lore and Language of Schoolchildren* by Iona and Peter Opie (Oxford, 1967)
8. *Jest Upon Jest* by John Wardroper (Routledge and Kegan Paul, 1970)
9. *An Apologie for Poetrie* by Sir Philip Sidney (London, 1595)
10. *Areopagitica* by John Milton (London, 1644)
11. *On Education* by John Locke (London, 1693)
12. *Goody Two Shoes* (John Newbery, London, 1766)
13. *A Little Pretty Pocket Book* (John Newbery, London, 1743)
14. *The Lilliputian Magazine or Children's Repository* (London, 1780)
15. *Some Account of the Author Tommy Trip and of his Dog Jouler* (John Newbery, London 1767)
16. *Autobiography* by Francis Place, edited by Mary Thale (Cambridge 1972)
17. *The Familiar Letter Writer* (Francis Newbery, London 1788)
18. *What Katy Did Next* by Susan Coolidge (1886)
19. *Rising at Darkingdale* by Sheila Dunnett (London, 1974)
20. *Psalm 62, Verse 9*
21. *The Secret Garden* by Frances Hodgson Burnett (London 1911)
22. *Old Fashioned Children's Books* edited by A. W. Tuer

(reprinted Evelyn Adams and Mackay, 1969)
23 Quoted in *Class Struggle and the Industrial Revolution* by John Foster (Weidenfeld and Nicolson, 1974)
24 *Life and Adventures of Michael Armstrong the Factory Boy* by Frances Trollope (London, 1840)
25 Quoted in *Written for Children* by John Rowe Townsend (Pelican, 1976)
26 *Alan Quartermain* by H. Rider Haggard (London, 1887)
27 *The Gorilla Hunters* by R.M. Ballantyne (London, 1861)
28 Essay in *The Thorny Paradise* by Geoffrey Trease, edited by Edward Blishen (Kestrel, 1975)
29 *The Princess and Curdie* by George MacDonald (London, 1882)
30 Launched in *Magnet* Magazine, by Frank Richards in 1908.
31 *The Times*, March 13th, 1974.

What were we arguing about?

It was at a publisher's reception, one of those evenings which, whatever the organiser's original purpose, serve to bring together old friends and enemies to talk about life and the sparks that fly upwards.

A group of authors discussed *the* new problem, or rather the old problem in its new guise: pressure to produce children's books free of the old assumptions about class, colour, sex. Well, yes, some agreed that the conventional writer's stockpot had got a bit stale, today's readership was much broader than yesterday's, times had changed, life had moved on and all writers, children's authors particularly, had to move with it.

Then the conversation veered into choppier waters. Words like 'formula writing', 'didactic', 'social engineering' were heard, and even more emotive: *outside interference.* Said one: 'You cannot write to order. It comes from inside or not at all.'

Broad, passionate declarations like this are not to be contradicted, but I was rash enough to mutter something to the effect that it did no harm for writers to pay heed to others.

I got no further: 'Well, of course you say that. You're a committed writer anyway.'

There was no reply to that. Not that I'm normally at a loss for words, but right at that moment an idiotic picture came into my mind, accompanied by this caption: 'Found guilty, he was committed to Newgate and dragged cursing from the dock.'

Committed and cast out. And by commitment separated from the world (joys and cares) of creativity, imagination, fantasy, humour, tragedy, the tongue of fire and the beat of the flying horse's wings, condemned to formula writing of didactic content for the purpose of social engineering.

I dragged myself away from the conversation, not cursing so much as brooding, as you do when the apt reply evades you until three o'clock the next morning.

When people counterpose commitment and creativity, often enough they are thinking of a commitment to social change, in this case to further the rights of working-class, black or female children. The new, even when about to be justified, excites hostility, while the old, even when about to be discarded, is tolerated on the inertia principle. The rule may rule even though, as Brecht shrewdly noted, it ought to be thought exceptional.

The status quo has its magic, appearing to be 'life' when it is clinging on for dear life. And many writers have a deep attachment to the status quo. Fear of change is a powerful stimulus to creative escapism, back into the past, back into childhood, away into never-never land. Who wants to grow up/older? Who says the future will be better than the past? And when to natural fears are added less agreeable fears of loss of privilege, impressive forces are at work.

You are attached to the status quo, you commit yourself to change. Attachment to the past, the present even, calls up the deepest instincts, commitment to the future calls for an act of thought, an act of faith in one's thought.

Deeply rooted conventional attitudes, traditionally accepted outlooks speak to us with an unconscious air of authority. The Christian writers of children's stories can speak of the 'triumph of the light over the dark', quite unaware of how controversial a statement that is, the author of books reflecting a very limited middle-class background and experience can tell you with utter honesty: 'I am not concerned with class, only with people.'

So with other things: the Englishman, safe behind frontiers almost inviolate for a millenium, marvels at the lack of a sense of humour in foreigners, the decent white is entirely bewildered by the touchiness of the black, and the male comedian stares blankly when asked, 'Why no jokes about fathers-in-law?'

These attitudes lie deep down in that well of the mind below the conscious activity of the everyday. The water lies so low we have forgotten when and where the rain fell that fed it, do not know through how many strata it has seeped and what it has absorbed on its way down. This is the level to which we all go when we dream, from which writers draw their most spontaneous work, so surprising even themselves at times that they are persuaded their inspiration has no earthly, material source.

Certainly they think it is not to be calculated or quantified, to be analysed only with difficulty, not to be disputed, and not — perish the thought — guided or organised.

Yet here, say writers, are people, non-writers at that, who reckon they can change by an act of will relations of human beings across the divides of society, colour or sex, as writers see them. They think they can replace the rainfall in the well by bucketsful from the tap, meticulously cleansed of social contamination.

Well, there's a clear antagonism between reformers and writers, many writers at least. But what of the 'committed' writers? Where do they stand? Do they — from the conviction that people, deprived, dominated, oppressed, neglected, scorned, condescended to, should have justice — imagine it can be done between the covers of a book, by deliberate decision, here and now? And if they do, and act on the conviction, will what they write be literature, will it be *the story*? Will it draw the kids from play and the old folk from the chimney corner? Will it cause pleasure or will it only command respect?

Such are those writers' questions.

There are some, non-writers, and for them I have more than a sneaking sympathy, who will answer: so what? Who are the writers anyway, that they should seek exemption from the demands of the time, a special law of human conduct for themselves, enabling them to ignore in the name of art what is going on around them?

Indeed, indeed. And some writers will reply defiantly: I shall write what I like, and believe it, though that has never been entirely true, at any time or anywhere. Some writers will feel guilty (which is quite easy for writers even though they appear arrogant on the surface) but they will go on with what they are doing, hoping that this is a new fashion (are pony books going out or coming in again?) and one they can live through with reasonable cunning.

Yet others will turn the question round again and say: You are against the old stereotypes of plot, setting, character. Who isn't? But, if you drive us too hard you will only get a new set of stereotypes, butch women, nice blacks, bosses with fangs. If that satisfies you, go ahead: by all means replace the mediocre books of reactionary content with mediocre books of progressive content — but don't call it literature.

So the debate goes on, each side misrepresenting the other now and then, a debate rendered more acrimonious by people who, finding life not exciting enough as it is, are spreading it abroad that after the passing of the Sex Discrimination Act anyone found portraying a girl character crying or wearing an apron will immediately be sent to break stones on Dartmoor.

Ah, but nothing so drastic is going to happen. Not even people like myself, who are mildly optimistic about the new laws, have such wild hopes that the legislature is about to free us of our critical and self-critical tasks and release us for purely creative activity.

But something has already happened. What is noticeable these past few years, is that everyone has been set to brooding about their own work. The grit has been at work in the oyster and while so far we have had mostly expressions of discomfort, there are pearls in the making. Publishers' editors have looked for or been obliged to look for a wider range of authors and illustrators, to think about new series. Existing authors have responded to the new situation with modern work, serious and comic.

The conventional restrictions on girl characters in particular have been put aside by many authors. Girls in children's books now move with a freedom and decisiveness not often seen before. There's a long way to go, but the situation is opening up. It is only in the present climate that I myself would have had the nerve to attempt a book around a female character, for I have found the conventional demands of the past impossible to comply with.

Even better have been the new insights into history. A list I prepared first some two years ago, in response to readers' requests for historical children's novels reflecting popular life rather than kings in oak trees, has grown to over forty titles and is added to almost by the month.

The efforts to respond to the challenge of the immigrant community's children, though still having a long way to go, are not to be despised.

Many writers have responded, even if their reaction to the situation is to retreat into the cobwebby realms of alleged fantasy. I say 'alleged' because, in the kind of book I'm thinking of, the author imagines fantasy has no rules and can mean what he says it means.

No writer has been unaffected. My own work deeply so, and I have been forced to think hard about the new imperatives. Are they indeed an imposition on writers or are they pointers in a new direction? Are they abstractions or are they a new light on reality? More specifically are writers being invited to show people as they ought to be (the ideal) rather than as they are ('life')? If this latter were the case, then most writers would decline the invitation, as they have done similar invitations in the past.

Or, are writers being invited not only to inspect again their own world, which they thought they knew but which has rapidly and irrevocably changed, but also a new world of whose existence they barely knew?

If this is so, and I believe as a writer that it is, then it is an invitation writers should respond to, not as a social duty, but as a welcome shaft of light in the mind or, to go back to the analogy of the well, a sudden access of flood water.

Our world has changed. I remember the sense of comfort I used to get as a kid when the teacher pointed to the map and said: 'There is our country, you will always find it in the centre.' What marvellous good fortune, though I could never work out why I was so lucky to have been born just north of centre of the country that was the centre of the world. I accepted it, though, as simply as I accepted the proposition that the world was a sphere. Only later did I find out, from a geography teacher with a sense of humour, that not only is every country at the 'centre' of the globe, but that different projections of maps show different countries in different sizes. You could make India, China, the Soviet Union expand or contract at will.

No more though. These days the most insular of Britons knows, if only through the Olympic Games, that the world has changed. The world to which Britons went out, now comes to them. How innocent to imagine that you could pump the wealth out of other countries without drawing part of the population with it. The Romans discovered this and, unable to bear it, declined and fell. Why should we follow them, if we can change or, even for a start, begin to see with new eyes?

We do not have to write works of international scope to reflect modern change (which incidentally even puts the animal world in turmoil — how do *The Gorilla Hunters* and *Call of the Wild* stand now in the light of our new wisdom?). Every story — the school story, the historical novel, the comic — has undergone a change while our fingers are on the home keys. To *ignore* the change surely requires an act of will, or wilfulness.

I must refer here to my own writing, for it represents to me an experience others may recognise, that of the problem which is its own solution. My chief ambition since I began to write children's books, and many years before that, was to write books in which ordinary children — children from working-class homes, from the estates, from a background like my own — might recognise themselves, yet feel the vicarious excitement for which convention deems characters from a class apart to be necessary. For I believe that only when we have a body of literature which truly reflects its whole readership, in realist and escapist terms, can we say we are not concerned with class any more, but only with people.

Well, as it has turned out, my stories have expanded their range, aiming at the free girl character, the black, too. It sounds like your ready-made formula writing. But here's roughly what happened, or part of it.

Writers know that writing is sometimes like launching a boat from a sticky patch of mud. You know roughly where you want to go but can't get started, though you push and shove the boat and occasionally stop to walk around and give it a kick.

At some point, though, it starts to move, gathers momentum, the once intractable object gets a life of its own and drags you with it. At last you feel yourself lucky to jump in and grab for the tiller.

I wanted to write an Elizabethan story of an apprentice who discovers that his fortune depends on sailing on a slave ship, who sets the slaves free and at last sails home a grown man in the company of Drake. It was a worthy notion and I sweated over it. But at first it would not budge. Then I read a memoir by Drake's nephew about his uncle's raid on the treasure trains in the Caribbean. Drake's allies were the Cimaroons, he said, escaped slaves who lived as guerillas in the rain forest. Then I realised that was the intractable element in my story. It was the slaves or rather my own prejudiced view of them as people to be pitied and set free. As people who claimed their own freedom, they stood out suddenly in my mind as real characters. Instead of their being simply factors in the story of my hero, he became a factor in their story. The tensions thus created, the energy released, made the story begin to move. But the new element was not invented, it was no abstraction. It was simply a part of reality, of history, that I had hitherto ignored and might have gone on doing so but for the imperative to look again at what I had previously accepted.

A little later I tried, for the third or fourth time, to write a school story. It had to be a comprehensive school of course. The dominance of the private school story is more or less gone, thank goodness. But with it has gone the conveniently enclosed scene which gives the school community a life of its own. A state school story has really to be a community story, as parents, police, others intrude on the daily life of the pupils. Comprehensive school stories (some critics' illusions to the contrary) are thus less likely material for formula stories than the old boarding-school set-up.

I had in mind a boy who has problems which arise from his

Front-cover picture for the *Third Class Genie*.

background, housing, and so on, as well as problems from his personal relations at school. He enlists the aid of fantasy to solve them. Fantasy is highly appropriate to the working-class story, for indeed many of the problems suffered by the poorer families seem at first sight to be susceptible only of fantasy solutions. Anyway, I had my hero. I had his problems. I had a bully waiting for him at school. I had a genie waiting to help him out (perhaps).

But the story stayed stuck. Then I heard my own children discussing the way some of the West Indian pupils threw their weight about at school and why. Another character leapt uninvited into my story, a West Indian and a bully. It hardly seemed Race Relations orientated, but that was exactly how it proved to be, for now the hero had a choice of bullies, a black one he feared and white one he detested but who cynically offered to protect him from the first. I felt the boat moving.

It was only half way through the story that something hit me which I had been quite blind to. The genie, too, was black. Not because I made him black, but because genies are black.

A good deal of the magic of European and Arab civilisation has been made by the labour of black genies. It wasn't insight on my part, simply hindsight. Once the genie materialised, he did so into the tensions already existing not only in my story but in every real school and community in the country.

Into the story, also uninvited, came a strong girl character, not by intention but by observation, for as every city teacher knows, girls from West Indian families are just not to be pushed around.

There's a good deal more to tell (who can stop a writer talking?) but to sum up, my experience has been that seen as an abstraction the question of removing bias from children's books can be a burden to writers. Seen as an index of the enormous changes which have taken place and continue to take place in the world around us, it marks an opportunity. There has never been such a wealth of characters, such diverse motivation, such complexity of personal problems calling for reflection in our stories. These are not the conditions which will impel writers to stereotyped or formula writing. On the other hand, these diverse elements in themselves do not lead to creative complexity in the work of any writer, even the writers most willing to draw on them, the ones called 'committed'!

For them the problems are several. There is impatience, the desire to solve a social problem within a book and thus stimulate the reader to solve it in reality, or the impulse to state the problem in its starkest terms and provide a similar stimulus. Then there is the confusion between the fairly precisely controlled business of analysis, which goes with a social critique, and the not so precisely controlled business of creating a fictional world in which the people have their own life.

There is worse: apprehension at being found inadequate in the reflection of the social scene and coming up last of all like the US cavalry, a cloud of anxiety at the thought of being found inadequate as a purveyor of *literature.* Myself, I would rather face the former apprehension than the latter anxiety, for social criteria are at least disputable, while the verdict of the critic whose only standards are 'literary' is like Humpty Dumpty's definition of a word and just as unanswerable.

To guide myself down this vale of tears, trying to meld the impulse to tell a story with the desire to change the world, I've made myself a number of golden rules, bearing in mind what Bernard Shaw said — that the first golden rule is there are none.

1. A novel is a story about people with problems, not about problems looking for people to happen to. Good intentions don't make a story thrilling or funny — but then everything from a joke to a spontaneous act of heroism has a point.

2. No character, however fantastic, can be imagined unless its prototype exists in the real world outside. It's a matter of seeking, finding, claiming and transforming.

3. What a book has to say (its message?) should come out in the action rather than the statement. Action too determines character. The words *motive* and *motion* have the same root.

4. Follows from three. Love thine enemy, at least to the extent of letting him act out his case. Children can judge by actions. They know the good can sometimes be as hard as the bad, and they know all about the grey area in between where they spend a lot of time themselves.

5. There are no simple choices. Ask any child who has the chance to stop some obnoxious bullying by telling teacher

whether life's a straight knock-down fight between good and evil.

There are more, and no doubt others could supplement or dispute these, for they by no means explore all the problems that arise in writing about today's world for today's children. I suspect, though, that the rules are not so very different from those any writer might work out, whether he considers himself 'committed' or not.

So, what were we arguing about at the beginning?

FURTHER READING
Books which attempt a realistic picture of ordinary people

Richard Armstrong, *Sabotage at the Forge* (Dent), *Sea Change* (Dent/Knight), *The Mystery of Obadiah** (Dent)
Gillian Avery, *A Likely Lad* (Collins/Lions)
Martin Ballard, *Dockie* (Longman Young Books/Lions)
Nina Bawden, *Carrie's War* (Gollancz/Puffin), *The Peppermint Pig* (Gollancz/Puffin)
Leila Berg, *A Box for Benny* (Brockhampton), *Bouncing* (and others in the *Nippers* series), (Macmillan), *Little Pete Stories* (Methuen/Puffin)
Hester Burton, *No Beat of Drum* (Oxford University Press), *Time of Trial* (Oxford University Press)
Peter Carter, *The Black Lamp* (Oxford University Press), *The Gates of Paradise,* (Oxford University Press)
Winifred Cawley, *Gran at Coalgate* (Oxford University Press)
Catherine Cookson, *Joe and the Gladiator* (Macdonald/Puffin), *The Nipper* (Macdonald/Puffin)
Gordon Cooper, *An Hour in the Morning* (Oxford University Press), *A Time in the City* (Oxford University Press)
Audrey Coppard, *Nancy of Nottingham* (Heinemann)
Marjorie Darke, *A Question of Courage* (Kestrel)
Esther Forbes, *Johnny Tremain* (Longman Young Books)
Frederick Grice, *The Bonny Pit Laddie* (Oxford University Press), *The Luckless Apple* (Oxford University Press)
E.W. Hildick, *Jim Starling* (and others in the same series), (Chatto and Windus)
Eric Houghton, *They Marched with Spartacus** (Brockhampton)
Charles Israel, *Who was then the Gentleman?** (Macmillan)
Robert Leeson, *The Demon Bike Rider* (Collins/Lions), *The Third Class Genie* (Lions), *Maroon Boy* (Collins)
Marget Lovett, *Jonathan* (Faber and Faber)
Allan Campbell Maclean, *Hill of the Red Fox* (Collins/Lions), *Master of Morgana* (Collins/Lions), *The Year of the Stranger* (Collins/Lions)
Margaret Potter, *Smoke Over Shap* (BBC Publications)

Susan Price, *Twopence A Tub* (Faber and Faber)
William Rayner, *Big Mister* (Collins)
Geoffrey Trease, *Bows Against the Barons* (Brockhampton), *The Runaway Serf* (Hamish Hamilton)
Walter Unsworth, *Whistling Clough* (Gollancz/Puffin)
Stanley Watts, *The Breaking of Arnold* (Longman Young Books/Topliners)

* possibly available in some libraries

Other books in the **Papers on Children's Literature** series edited by the Children's Rights Workshop include:

Sexism in Children's Books:
Facts, figures and guidelines

The articles collected in this booklet analyse sexism in children's books and present powerful statistical evidence of its frequency and range. The McGraw-Hill Guidelines show how to begin to recognise and combat sexism in literature and in the use of language.

p/b 60p
ISBN 0 904613 22 4

Racist and Sexist Images in Children's Books

The anti-racist articles in this pamphlet provide a starting point for debate and for developing challenges to racist attitudes. Various well-known children's books, including Charlie and the Chocolate Factory, Sounder and Dr Dolittle receive criticism for their images of Black people and the Black experience. Sexist attitudes are also discussed; the description of children's books from China provides a positive example for the fight against sex-stereotyping.

45p
ISBN 0 904613 09 7

Coming soon:

Little Miss Muffet Fights Back
An annotated bibliography of non-sexist children's books for all ages; also covering alternative publishing and children's books from The People's Republic of China.

p/b 75p
ISBN 0 904613 38 0

Children's Books in Multi-racial Britain
A collection of essays from people involved with children and books in multi-racial Britain. The points of view of the teacher, the writer, the librarian, etc. are covered.

p/b 75p
ISBN 0 904613 39 9